◆ Plain Prayers ◆
in a
Complicated World

Also by Avery Brooke

LEARNING AND TEACHING
CHRISTIAN MEDITATION
(Originally published as
HOW TO MEDITATE WITHOUT
LEAVING THE WORLD)

TRAILING CLOUDS OF GLORY:
Spiritual Values in Children's Books;
with Madeleine L'Engle.

FINDING GOD IN THE WORLD:
Reflections on a Spiritual Journey

• PLAIN PRAYERS •
IN A
COMPLICATED WORLD

by Avery Brooke
With Art by Robert Pinart

COWLEY PUBLICATIONS

Cambridge ◆ *Boston*
Massachusetts

Published in the United States of America
by Cowley Publications, a division of the Society
of St. John the Evangelist. No portion of this book
may be reproduced, stored in, or introduced into a retrieval system,
or transmitted, in any form or by any means
— including photocopying —
without the prior written permission
of Cowley Publications, except in the case of brief
quotations embodied in critical
articles and reviews.

Publishing History

A few of the prayers in PLAIN PRAYERS IN A COMPLICATED
WORLD originally appeared in YOUTH TALKS WITH GOD
(Scribners, 1959). Others were first published in PLAIN PRAYERS
FOR A COMPLICATED WORLD (Reader's Digest Press, 1975). A
number of the previously published prayers have appeared in *The
Reader's Digest, Weavings: A Journal of the Christian Spiritual Life,*
and many anthologies. A major proportion are new to this book.

Library of Congress Cataloging-in-Publication Data

Brooke, Avery
    Plain prayers in a complicated world / by
Avery Brooke with art by Robert Pinart.
        p. cm.
    Includes index.
    ISBN 1-56101-084-7
    1. Prayers. I. Title.
BV245.B6735   1993   93-22817
242'.8—dc20

This book is printed on acid-free paper and was produced in the
United States of America.

Cowley Publications
28 Temple Place
Boston, MA 02111

For my friend Maria West

TABLE OF CONTENTS

Acknowledgements

I would like to acknowledge with gratitude the patient and creative help and encouragement given me by my friend Jeannie Sandoval in putting together this book. Cynthia Shattuck of Cowley Publications is one of the wisest editors I know and I owe her my gratitude. She and Jeff McArn not only gave me good advice but the freedom to provide them with camera ready copy which enabled Robert Pinart and I to do the many small adjustments needed when producing a book of interrelated art and text.
I would also like to thank my friend Nelson Kane for his early guidance on the book's design. We didn't always take his advice, but without it we would never have gotten started. And without Brian Gockley, who ably set the type for us, we would have been unable to bring the book to completion.
Above all I would like to thank Robert Pinart who, when I asked if he would do 20 little pen and inks to be repeated on scattered pages, insisted on giving me wonderful drawings for almost every page.

Avery Brooke

PREFACE

The Christian Celts had a word that ties together the three quite different sections of this book — *to sain*. To sain meant to bless or baptize a secular or pagan custom into the church. The Celtic Church sained the activities of their daily lives and many of the old Celtic festivals. Today we stand in need of building similar bridges between the Christian church and an increasingly secular culture. Above all we need to learn to express our faith to our friends, our families, our children, and ourselves in everyday words that reflect the world in which we live. The first section of this book, *Graces and Table Prayers*, was written in response to that need. We long today for a climate where family prayers might seem natural and possible. But the practice runs counter to both secular culture and much of family life today. Family members scatter to different jobs, sports, and activities, and meals together are less frequent than in a earlier age.

The very word *family* has come to mean a whole constellation of varied groupings, often of unrelated people. I have therefore included a large number of graces and prayers for holidays and other occasions when it is more likely that people are gathered together, and where introducing grace or table prayers comes more naturally. This also gives an opportunity to baptize what are primarily secular holidays into a spiritual context. I have tried to write these graces so that they are usable for young or old, and in varied circumstances but, as with all of the prayers in this book, it is my hope that people will freely adapt and go on to pray in their own words.

The section on *Prayers for Meetings* grew out of a long involvement in parish activities. Within the church prayers in traditional language seem natural, but there is often a need for open, honest prayers expressing our thoughts and feelings in the clearest possible words. While in *Graces and Table Prayers* I try to bring the church into the world, in *Prayers for Meetings* I try to bring the world — in the sense of ordinary words, understandings, and feelings — into the church. Strangely, this often makes God more visible than when we use prayers in traditional words. It is my hope that laity as well as clergy will find these prayers a resource and that they will inspire others both to write and pray in their own "ordinary words."

The section on *Personal Prayers* is the most basic in the book. If we are not in touch with God as individuals, any prayers we say around the dining table or in meetings will be empty. We ourselves and our personal lives must be baptized, must be sained, into a relationship with God before we may sain anyone or anything else. Again, my prayers are only meant to offer a starting place or a reminder for the reader. It is in our personal lives that we know most clearly that we live in a complicated world. Traditions are crumbling around us. It is a time of confusing, bewildering, and frightening change. It is a complicated world for everyone and it is a complicated world for Christians. Answers to either personal or wider problems do not come easily. It is a time where we long for traditional ways, but traditional ways often no longer fit easily into our complicated world. If we are to rebuild our lives and our world, even as it crumbles, we must each turn to Christ for help. These are large words for a book of simple prayers, but it is simple prayer we need.

Avery Brooke
Noroton, CT 1993

· GRACES AND TABLE ·
PRAYERS

⋅ A GRACE ⋅

We thank you, God, for this meal, for our lives,
for other people, for beautiful things, for
goodness, and for you.

· ANOTHER GRACE ·

Thank you, God, for life and for the food that sustains life. May we live in gratitude and joy and in the service of others.

· A BREAKFAST GRACE ·

Jesus, lord of the universe, we come to another day. Thank you for the night's rest and for this first meal of the day.

Come with us, Jesus, as we go about our work. Give us the strength to do it well and the love to share with those whom we see today. And, in the midst of our busyness, help us to remember you.

◆ A GRACE AT LUNCH ◆

O Christ, lift us out of the busyness of our lives
and the confusions of our minds. Refresh us
in this pause for lunch. Help us to see where
we are and to turn our lives towards your life.

· WHEN SOMEONE IS AWAY ·

We aren't all here for this meal, Jesus, and we ask your blessing on those who are absent as well as we who are present. Bless this meal and those who prepared it.

• A GRACE ON VACATION •

We've been looking forward to vacation for a long time, God. Now it is here and we are grateful. Help us to use it well and joyously. Bless this vacation meal and the new and old friends and the new and old places we will see.

· GRACE FOR A PICNIC ·

We ask your blessing, Lord, on this day, this
place, this meal, and us. We thank you for the
sense of freedom, relaxation, and happiness
that picnics bring. May we be refreshed in body
and spirit by this meal and this time together.

· FRIENDSHIP ·

O God, we thank you for our friends and all the
joys they have brought us. We thank you for the
happiness of sharing work and problems and
laughter and for the joy of adventuring and
learning together. We thank you for the chance
to love and be loved by those who know us as we
really are.

· FOR OUR FAMILY ·

We pray for our family, Lord: For those who
live in our home or close to us and for those
who live at a distance. Be with them, Lord,
keep them safe from harm, guide them in
what they should do, and help them grow to
know you more and more.

• FOR A DEPARTURE •

God, someone we love is leaving today and we will miss *her*. Keep *her* safe while *she* is gone. May the people that *she* meets add to *her* life and *she* to theirs. Whether in work or play, in safety or danger, on new paths or old, stay with *her* wherever *she* goes and whatever *she* does.

· A New Child in the Home ·

We welcome _____, God, to our home with
great joy and gratitude. Help us to make this
the best possible home for _____ as it is for
us.

· IN CELEBRATION ·

Gracious Lord, today is a special and joyous
day. As we enter into the festivities help us to
keep our hearts open to you and each other.
May we share our joy and gratitude as we
celebrate, and when we return to simpler days
may we be enriched by the meaning of today.

· A BIRTHDAY PRAYER ·

Thank you God for life and for _____'s life in particular. We rejoice in that life and thank you for _____. Bless this festive meal, _____ and us.

· A BLESSING ·

O Lord, bless all the people we love, at home
and far away. Guide them by night and by day
and keep them always under your loving care.

And, Lord, bless too the people we don't love
as we should. Teach us to understand them
and love them in spite of what we dislike about
them. And help us to forgive those who have
acted badly toward us and bless them, too.

· LOVING OUR NEIGHBOR ·

O Christ, when we do not understand our
neighbors, nor they us, help us to think more
about how we could understand them and less
about how they could understand us. May we
never let fear keep us from speaking or acting,
nor carelessness increase misunderstanding.

· FOR THE PEOPLE WHO LIVE ·
IN OUR HOUSE

You have gathered us together, God, and we
are grateful. We thank you for this place to
live, this meal we are about to eat, and our
companionship.

· THOSE WHO HAVE NO HOME ·

Jesus, when we come home at night and open our front door, help us to remember those who have no home to come to. When we sit down to eat our meal, help us to remember those who have no meal to eat. When we lie down on our beds at night, help us to remember those who have no bed.

And may our remembering, Lord, help us to help those who have no home, no meal, no bed.

· FOR PRISONERS ·

God, if sometimes we cannot do as we want and
it makes us angry, help us to remember the
thousands in prisons who can seldom do what
they want, who are miserable and afraid and far
away from home. O God, let them know you
and give them comfort, hope, and freedom
once again.

· For Teachers ·

Lord, we pray for teachers. Comfort them
when they are misunderstood. Strengthen
them when they must work under difficult
conditions. Refresh them when their hours
are long. Above all, Lord, help them to give
their pupils an infectious love of learning,
work, and excellence.

· THE TROUBLES OF OTHERS ·

God, help us to enter into the troubles of
others, know them as if they were our own,
and act accordingly.

• For Strangers •

God, when I am in need, or those I know and
love are in need, it is easy to ask for your help.
But it is more difficult to pray for strangers.
Even when I know they are in great trouble,
their needs seem very distant. Help me to
imagine how they feel so that I may pray for
them, not just with words but with my heart.

· DIFFERENCES ·

Father, they do not look like us or act like us,
and it is easy to stay away from them. Help us
to reach out the hand of friendship — even
when they do not trust us — and to remember
that they too are your children.

· As You Taught Us ·

O Christ, as you taught us:

Help us not only to be fair but to be
     generous.
Help us not only not to fight but to
     make peace.
Help us not only not to steal but to
     give.
Help us not only not to lie but to
     search for the truth.
Help us not only not to do wrong but
     to do right.
Help us not only not to harm those
     who harm us but to forgive
     and help them.
Help us not only to love you but to
     serve you.

· THE NEW YEAR ·

We ask your blessing, God, on the year that is past and the year to come. It is a fresh start for all of us, God. Help us to learn from both our mistakes and our successes, and to live in this coming year more nearly as you would have us live.

• MARTIN LUTHER KING •

Help us to remember, Lord, how strong love can be in the face of hate and intolerance. We thank you for Martin Luther King Jr., who gave his life while teaching us this lesson.

· FOR LEADERS ·

O God, help our leaders
to lead. Whether they are
ordinary people whom
others imitate, or the
heads of organizations or
countries, help them to
use their power well.
Don't let them get so full
of their own importance
they forget what they are
doing or so busy that they
forget you. Fill them with
so much love that they
can understand their
followers and make peace
with their enemies.

· PRESIDENTS OF OUR COUNTRY ·

We thank you, God, for the great presidents of
our country who saw us through difficult and
formative times. And we pray for our president
today that you will guide and strengthen *him* to
lead us with wisdom, strength and justice
through the difficult days of our time.

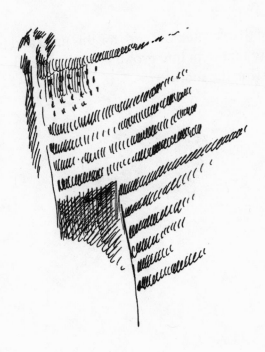

• A VALENTINE'S BLESSING •

O God of love, we celebrate today all the little
tokens of love that we have received
throughout the year. We thank you for the
friends and family who remember what is
important to us, the bit of help received with
work when we were tired and busy, the
unexpected compliment, the strangers who
were kind.

We thank you too, Lord, for this meal and the
care that went into growing, cooking, and
serving the food.

· ST. PATRICK'S DAY ·

God, the real Patrick is more exciting than the legend. Captured by Irish slave raiders from his home in England, when he was just a boy, he learned to pray and you helped him escape. Later, you called him back to bring Christianity to the Irish.

May we in our turn have the wisdom to pray and the courage to obey, as Patrick did.

· LENT ·

Lord Jesus, in these weeks when we remember your time of fasting and temptation in the desert, help us to better learn to find and love you in our neighbor, recognize and serve you in your creation, and hear and follow you in Scripture.

· We Have Been Wasteful ·

Lord, we have been wasteful. We have loved ease and luxury and more to eat than is good for us. And now the world is running out of everything.

Forgive us, Lord, and teach us how to change our ways, to care for the earth you made, and to learn how to give everyone what they need.

• EASTER •

O God, we thank you for rebirth — for forgiveness, and for second chances for people and nations. This Easter season, as sleeping seeds and trees begin to burst into new life, help us too to grow more alive and more nearly into the people you designed us to be.

· RESURRECTION ·

We thank you, Christ, for
giving a home to all those
who have gone before us
and for being there to
welcome them. Help
us to live in that
knowledge and
prepare in faith
for our own
home –
coming.

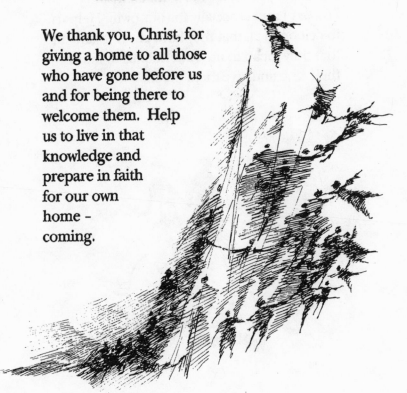

· MOTHERS OR FATHERS ·

We thank you today, Lord, for all *Mothers*
(*Fathers*) and especially for our own. Help us
to celebrate all that they have given us and all
that they mean to us. And help us to know
their love and give them ours.

· MEMORIAL DAY ·

We remember today, God, all those people who have died and are now with you. We especially remember people who have fought and died for our country and others who have lived and worked to make our lives healthier and happier.

We remember too all those who were near and dear to us. They are still dear and we think of them with love. For all these people who are no longer with us, we thank you, God.

· The Fourth of July ·

Today we celebrate freedom and our country, Lord. We take the benefits of both too much for granted. Help us to realize our good fortune and celebrate this day with gratitude.

· OUR COUNTRY ·

O Christ, we love this land. We wish it were always a simple love and often it is, but life has become complicated. Good gets mixed up with evil, and mountains of laws and regulations and numbers and systems get in our way when we wish to make everything work as it should. When things go wrong it becomes easy to give up, to blame other people, and to do nothing.

O Christ, give us the unashamed courage to believe in the highest and the best ideals of our country, and enough passionate patience to make them come true.

· LABOR DAY ·

Today, in the midst of play, we celebrate work.
Thank you, God, for the work of others and
for the chance to work ourselves. Thank you
for this food and the work of the people who
grew and picked it. Thank you for those who
brought it to the market and those who sold it.
And thank you for the people who bought,
cooked, and served this meal.

· BACK TO SCHOOL ·

Jesus, tomorrow school starts for _____ and
_____. May *she* and _____ sleep well and
wake up with excitement as *she* looks forward
to seeing friends and learning new things. Be
with *her,* Jesus, and bring *her* home, safe and
happy.

• To Be Thankful •

We have many things to be thankful for, God,
and sometimes we remember them and other
times we forget. When something large or
small goes wrong, it fills our minds and we
forget those things for which — when we
remember — we are thankful. Help us to
remember the good things, God. To name
them, to savor them, and to be thankful to you.

· THANKSGIVING ·

We thank you, God, for this meal and for the
family and friends who share it. In the midst of
our plenty help us to remember those who have
little to be thankful for. And help us to help them.

· AS CHRISTMAS APPROACHES ·

Jesus, forgive us for being so busy, confused, and disorganized that we have little time to think of you as Christmas approaches. Help us to pause now and remember your coming to us and to the world.

• A CHRISTMAS GRACE •

Lord Jesus, today we celebrate your being born on earth many years ago. May you be reborn in our hearts this Christmas day.

· FOREVER AND EVER ·

Long before we were born or our mothers and
fathers were born or their mothers and fathers
were born, you were.

Before there were any people or any world you
were here.

And you made us with love and watched us
and picked us up when we fell and helped us
try again. And all our lives you will love us and
when we leave the world we will come home to
you. And our children and our children's
children will love you, and come home to you.
And your kingdom will always wait for us and
for all the people who ever were or ever will be.

· AMEN ·

O Father, may everything that you are become everything we want to be. May everything that we have said to you in love be remembered by us, now and always.

• PRAYERS FOR MEETINGS •

· BE WITH US AS WE MEET ·

O God, be with us as we meet. Open our
minds to mutual understanding, our hearts to
our common purpose, and our wills to fulfill
your will.

· NEITHER SUCCESS NOR FAILURE ·

O God, let neither success nor the desire for
success, failure nor the desire to avoid failure,
becloud our vision of what you want us to do.

· HELP US TO UNDERSTAND ·

O Holy Spirit, teacher of us all, be with us as
we meet. Help us to understand what we need
to understand, and see what we need to see.

· THE COURAGE TO SPEAK ·

O God, help us to have the courage to speak
when we fear we may be wrong, and the humility
not to mind when we are.

· What You Wish Us to Do ·

O God, open our minds that we may see what you wish us to do and then give us the will, the courage, the intelligence and the love to do it.

· In a Spirit of Freedom ·

Help us to inquire, debate, study and decide in a spirit of freedom and loving companionship in the sure knowledge that you are with us.

· Take Our Eagerness ·

Lord Jesus, take our eagerness, our confusion, our friendship, our difficulties and our imperfect love of you and, with your grace, forge of them something true to you and useful for ourselves and others.

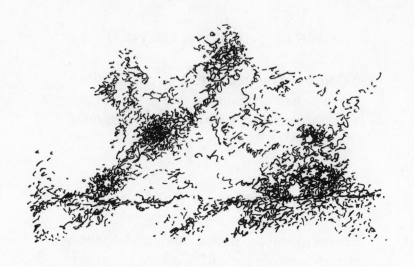

· THROUGH YOUR EYES ·

O God, may all that we see be seen through your
eyes, all that we hear be heard through your
ears, and all that we think and say be with the
guidance of your Spirit.

• Love and Practicalities •

Lord Jesus, help us to remember your love
while dealing with practicalities and
practicalities while caught up in loving you.

• And in the Days to Follow •

O Spirit of God, be with us today and in the
days to follow. Guide our thoughts, nurture
our feelings, and increase our understanding.

· AT A YOUTH GROUP ·

O Christ, the world is before us and we could do many things. Help us choose wisely where we should go and what we should do.

Sometimes we dream prideful dreams of being very important and having everyone look up to us, and other times we think we can't really do much of anything.

Help us to dream, Christ, but to dream good and possible dreams. Give us the courage to start living them, the humility to start at the bottom and the patience to keep on.

· STARTING SOMETHING NEW ·

O God, we are about to start something new. We believe that it is what you would like us to do. In our most confident moments we think that we can do it well, but sometimes we are not so sure.

You know the risks, God, and you know our weaknesses and our strengths. Keep us from confusion and guard us from either pride or fear. May we know the happiness of working together for you and the quiet joy of doing our best.

· PRECONCEPTIONS ·

O God, give us the strength to put aside our preconceptions and to think freely and clearly, using the minds that you have given us without the shackles of fear or prejudice.

· SO BUSY DOING GOOD WORKS ·

O God, help us not to become so busy doing good works that we forget to be Christian while doing them.

· TO SORT LIVING TRUTHS ·
FROM DYING CUSTOMS

O God, in this time of change and unrest, help
us to sort living truths from dying customs.
Help us to have the courage to look beyond the
expected and familiar ways and the humility to
recognize the wisdom of them.

· FAILURE ·

We worked hard, Lord, and it didn't come out
as we hoped. Help us to understand what
happened and why. And grant us, gracious
Lord, the courage and wisdom to plan what we
should do next.

· TO REORGANIZE ·

We need to reorganize, God, to change the
way we look at things and the way we function
and it is difficult. We are used to things as they
are and even when we know that we should
change, we are reluctant. Gracious God, help
us to see clearly how things are now, how they
might be, and how to get there.

· MONEY ·

Some people talk, Jesus, as if the church should
never mention money, as if money were
somehow unspiritual. But you spoke of money
often, and so must we. Help us, Lord, to learn
to speak of the church's need for money so
that people will understand and give. And
when we have money help us to spend it wisely.

• PLANNING FOR THE FUTURE •

Help us, Lord, to look at the past and present
so that we may better plan for the future, and to
face our strengths and weaknesses with honesty
and wisdom. Help us to be open to your
guidance as we discuss and plan for the future,
and grant us both generous imagination and
practical plans.

· To See Clearly ·

O God, help us to see clearly where we are, and where you would like us to be. Grant us the courage to share both dreams and realities.

And help us to have the humility to listen to you and to each other.

· DIFFICULT DECISIONS ·

We have to make some difficult decisions, Lord, and we need your help. Visit us with your compassion that we may be compassionate, and with your courage that we may face reality. And send us your Holy Wisdom that we may be wise.

• WHY WE ARE HERE •

O God, help us to know why we are here. There is not one of us that has such a pure and un-cluttered heart that there isn't a lot of furniture between us and the truth.

Help us to be simple today. To be honest. To be open. To listen.

Help us to put away pride and to talk of you and of ourselves with more courage than we think we have.

• THE IMPORTANT AND •
THE UNIMPORTANT

O God, help us to see the difference between the important and the unimportant. Let nothing block our vision by seeming vital when it is inconsequential or by seeming inconsequential when it is vital.

· As We Work Together ·

Gracious Lord, as we work together, help each one of us to be neither self centered nor falsely humble, but truthful. Help us to give of our best and to receive the best that others can give.

• OUR HEARTS AND MINDS •

O Christ, help us to understand you, not just intellectually, but in the living of our lives. Help us to bring our minds to bear on the problems in our hearts and our hearts to bear on the problems in our minds.

・ LISTEN TO EACH OTHER ・

O Christ, be with us in our inner uncertainties
and our outward confusions. Guide our gropings
for ways to express what each knows is important
but finds difficulty in communicating. Help us,
above all, to listen to each other — and through
each other, to listen to you.

· Help Us to See ·

Help us not to fool ourselves with words, God,
with talk of being sorry when we are not sorry,
with talk of sacrifice when we have no intention
of sacrificing, with talk of action when we are
too lazy to act.

Where our vision is dim, help us to see. Where
our hearts are imprisoned by fears, release
them. And when we see and feel your truth,
give us the courage to act.

• OUR CHURCH IS TORN APART •

O Christ, our church is torn apart. The things which should bring unity are bringing disunity. And those that should bring peace are bringing war. We who should love each other, are coming close to hate.

Show us the way out of conflict and how to come together once again in you and for you.

• CONFLICTS •

Lord Jesus, we have conflicts. Some of us believe strongly that we should do one thing and others believe strongly that we should do another. Help us, Lord, to understand each other's point of view. Save us from stubborn pride and open our hearts and minds to new ways of seeing and new solutions.

· THIS TIME OF WORKING ·
TOGETHER

O God, we thank you for this time of working
together. We are grateful for the witness that
each of us has been to the other, for the living
knowledge that this has given us of what your
church is and of how our individual
weaknesses, when offered to you in humility,
are received back as a common strength. May
this joyful knowledge of our oneness in
redemption remain with us in the coming
months and be used for the furtherance of
your kingdom.

· A JOB COMPLETED ·

Most gracious God, we give you thanks that
what we had planned and worked for for so
long has come to pass. Help us to remember
to be grateful.

• EVANGELISM •

Help us, Christ, to have the courage, grace, and
ability to witness to you for those who need you
but find faith difficult. Help us talk with those
who see you as an intellectual proposition to be
argued instead of a person who loves them.
Teach us what to say to those who see church
services as full of empty nonsense. Show us how
to witness to those who believe the church should
be full of perfect people.

And help us, Christ, to show them what you mean
to us by the way we live as well as by what we say.

· AN ECUMENICAL GATHERING ·

O God, we thank you for the gift of Christian
diversity and for this opportunity to observe and
cherish different ways of Christian perception,
love and action.

• A BIBLE STUDY •

Teach us, Lord, how to read the Bible. Help us to hear you speak to us today through the words written and spoken long ago. Guide the perceptions of our minds and the understanding of our hearts so that we will hear what you wish us to hear and learn what you wish us to learn.

• OUTREACH •

Lord Jesus, as we reach out to help others in your name, we need your help to do it well. Give us determination to overcome obstacles and courage to face the unfamiliar. Grant us patience with those whose ways are not our ways and compassionate imagination so that we know how people feel. Teach us to give help, Lord, without giving offense.

• GRACE FOR A CHURCH SUPPER •

Gracious Lord, we ask your blessing on this gathering of your people. We thank you for each and every one of us, and for the church community that you have given to us all. We thank you for this meal and for those who have prepared it.

⋅ For a New Leader ⋅

Lord, we ask your blessing on _____ who
has been appointed (*elected*) as the new leader
(*chair*, *director*) of _____. May he (*she*) be
empowered to lead us with diligence,
understanding, and patience.

· A PRAYER GROUP ·

O Holy Spirit, teacher of prayer, be with us today. Help each of us to find in one another's words or questions whatever it is that we should learn. And when we go from here, help us to make it our own.

◆ FOR A QUIET DAY ◆

O Christ, be with us today in silence and in speech. Clear out our minds of busyness and worry, and open them to hear your voice.

· TEACH US THE WAYS OF PEACE ·

Christ, no one on earth really wants the pain
and horror of war. We do not want to kill or
to be killed, to hurt or to be hurt. But we all
see injustice, and sometimes it makes us angry
and we see no other way to right the wrong
except by war. Christ, teach us the ways of
peace! Calm our angry hearts and grant to all
peoples and their leaders unending patience
in the search for peace and justice. Help us to
be ready to give up some of our comforts and
power and pride, so that war will leave the face
of the earth and we may work for you in peace.

· THE SMALL THINGS ·

Lord, we know that we are unable to do great things for you, but help us to be neither too lazy nor too proud to do the small things.

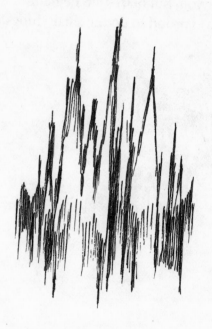

◆ ACCEPT OUR WORK ◆

O God, where our knowledge is insufficient
and our ability inadequate, accept our work in
the spirit given and redeem it for your use.

◆ OUR CHURCH ◆

Thank you, God, for bringing together so
many people who love you. Help us to pray
and sing as if with one voice and to lose our
differences in remembering you.

⋅ PERSONAL PRAYERS ⋅

· A MORNING PRAYER ·

Take my hand, Lord, and lead me through this
day, step by step. Remind me that I cannot do
everything I wish, nor do any of it perfectly.
Only you are perfect, and only with your help
can I do my best. Help me to remember to ask
for that help.

• When God Seems Far Away •

O God, when all the world looks gray and dirt shows everywhere and nothing is as it should be, you seem very far away.

O God, help me when I feel like this. Help me to remember the days when you were near and I knew it. Even when you seem far away, help me never to turn my back on you. Set me on the path to you and help me hold fast until I find your light once more.

• Time to Pray •

Jesus, I can't expect to get to know you if I seldom speak with you. Help me to find the time and place to pray every day.

• A DIFFICULT DECISION •

God, I don't know what to do. Obviously whatever I decide, it will make a great difference. I have gathered all the information I need. I have weighed those things for and against. I have asked the advice of experts and friends, and I still don't know what to do.

Help me, God, to choose wisely. And once I have chosen, help me to go forward in faith.

• OUR CULTURE •

What we should say or do, Christ, is no longer
clear. Not so long ago the lines were sharply
drawn. Now it seems as if no line is clear, rules
are an invitation to do something else and
customs change as fast as the weather.

Grant me the grace to see things as you see
them, Christ, and the strength and courage to
live in your light.

• I FEEL ANGRY AND HURT •

Everything seemed fine, God. I did the very best I could and I felt happy about it. But no one cares and I feel angry and hurt.

I think that they have been unfair to me. Perhaps they have, God, and perhaps they haven't, but in either case I need to understand. Help me to think clearly, to act wisely and not to hold a grudge.

· BEWILDERED ·

O Lord, when I am bewildered and the world
is all noise and confusion around me and I
don't know which way to go and am frightened, then be with me. Put your hand on my
shoulder and let your strength invade my
weakness and your light burn the mist from my
mind. Help me to move forward with faith in
the way I should go.

• FOR SOMEONE VERY SICK •

God, someone I love is very sick. *He* is in pain and I cannot help. *He* may even die, and I am afraid. O Father, you who made us all, take away *his* pain and make *him* well!

And renew both *his* spirit and mine so that we may better love and serve you.

• GOD, MAKE ME WELL •

O God, I have been sick a long time and almost
forgotten how it feels to be well. The doctors do
their best but they take a very long time. Help
me to be as cheerful as I can so that my family
are not too unhappy. And, O God, please make
me well, so that my body can feel full of joy and I
can work and play and get tired and sleep and
wake up happy.

• ADDICTION •

It's got hold of me, God, and I'm powerless to
stop it. It crept up on me when I wasn't
looking and became part of my being. I
thought that surely I could manage on my own.
I tried this way and that but nothing worked,
and I'm beaten.

I need help, Jesus, yours and the help of
others. Bring me through, Lord Jesus, to a new
and brighter place.

· TO KNOW MYSELF ·

I'm sorry, God, for many things I've done and haven't done. To know that you forgive me gives me joy. But tell me, God, what else you see that I don't. Tell me what is good about me as well as what needs change. Help me to know myself as I am, and see more clearly how you wish me to be.

· THE END OF THE WORLD ·

O God, help me to worry less about the end of the world, or the end of my life, or terrible things that may happen tomorrow, so that I may live to the full each moment of today.

· To Learn What Really · Matters

Christ, sometimes I feel guilty about things I should not feel guilty about. The "good" behavior I was taught is not always important or even good in your eyes. Help me to learn what really matters to you, Christ, and what does not.

· LITTLE THINGS ·

Lord, help me with little things that I forget. Remind me of the compliment that I should give, the letter to the friend I miss, the love I meant to express.

And when there are little things I want to do but shouldn't, hold me back. Help me to stop the cutting word, the boast, the scorn, the unkind laugh. In all these things, O Lord, help me to remember always how the other person feels and to act in love towards them.

• MARRIAGE •

I'm glad I'm married, Lord, but it isn't always easy. Help us then, Lord, to say what is on our hearts and minds in a way that the other can hear. And help each of us to listen.

Give me patience, Lord, when I should be patient and courage to speak out in disagreement when it is important. And remind me to do those little things which sometimes make all the difference.

· MY CHILDREN ·

Thank you, God, for my children. I know that
sometimes I lose patience with them and
sometimes I feel despair but underneath I have
deep love, caring, tenderness, and joy, and I
think they know that. Thank you for my
children, God. Keep them safe from harm and
help me to give them what they need.

• FOR GROWN CHILDREN •

It's hard to let go, God. For years I was trying to guide and teach and nurture my children and now they are independent. Whatever good I did or didn't do, and whatever mistakes I made or didn't make, are in the past.

Teach me how to love them as adult friends, as people in their own right with whom I can share and laugh and cry, knowing always that if they need me or I need them, we are here for each other.

Take care of my children, God, and do for them what I can no longer do.

· WHEN WORK IS HEAVY AND · DULL

A while ago my work seemed right to me, God. It challenged me and satisfied me and I was happy in it. But now it seems heavy and dull and long. I feel half alive when I work and surely this is not what you wish.

Help me to have the courage to change what is open to change and do what I must with lightness of heart.

· I'VE LOST MY JOB ·

I know that it isn't my fault, God, but I feel as if it were. And I'm frightened. Will I be able to find another job? All the securities and responsibilities of my life are threatened. Help me, God. Help me to know who I am and what I can do, and to speak and act with such confidence in that knowledge that a new way will open for me.

· DISCOURAGED ·

Christ, I am discouraged. I've worked and
worked. I've tried new ways. I've thought
about this problem till I've ached with
weariness. I've discussed it with those who
might help. And I don't know what to do
next. Christ, help me to see your will and
your way and give me the strength to follow
through.

· HATE ·

Jesus, I am full of hate. I feel deeply hurt and unfairly treated. I am bitter and angry. I feel like hitting out, like sweeping someone from the face of the earth.

Jesus, you who know what human pain and hurt feel like, who felt hatred, ridicule, and rejection, you who died alone, deserted by your friends but still felt and spoke love, help me to transform my bitterness and change my heart so that I may understand and love.

· A SIMPLER LIFE ·

Life has gotten confusing, complex, and full of pressures, God. I am pulled this way and that by too many demands and desires.

It is impossible to be my best self in the midst of this. Yet it is also hard to know how to make life simpler.

Help me to choose, God. Everything I do seems like something I should do, and yet I know that if I do not stop doing some things I will be able to do nothing well.

And if I do not leave some peace and quiet to listen to you, I will fail you, myself, and others.

· GOOD YET QUIET TIMES ·

When I am full of joy or pain, it is easy to remember you, Lord, and to thank you or ask your help. But there are some good yet quiet times when I never think of you. Times when work is hard but goes well, when friends are friends, when members of the family are together in quietness and love, when I have a chance to rest and be peaceful.

I thank you for these times, Lord. Help me to remember you then.

· SELF CONSCIOUSNESS ·

O God, I'm going to see a lot of people and I'm afraid I'll be wearing the wrong clothes, say the wrong thing, and act the wrong way. I'm afraid no one will like me, and way down deep I'm afraid someone will laugh at me.

Help me to forget what others think of me and lose myself in getting to know them, enjoy them and love them.

· WHEN ANGRY WITH A FRIEND ·

O Father, I am very angry with my friend and I don't want to be. Help me to calm my anger before I say or do the wrong thing. Show me why *he* acted the way he did and help me understand *him*.

If I did something wrong, help me to know it and say I'm sorry. If I did nothing wrong, help me to be patient and forgive *him*.

• WHEN I HAVE LOST MYSELF •

O God, I thank you for the place where no one goes but you and I, for the secret field, the tree, the rock, the corner in the house, where I may go and find myself again and, in finding me, find you.

What longed-for peace creeps in upon my heart, when, hidden in this secret place, I listen to the silence and slowly lose that tightness that held me fast, unhappy and afraid!

In time I find I can look around at your quiet things, the leaf so very near my head, the lines on the board beneath my feet or the bird that scolds a bit because I'm here and flies away. And when I've looked at those awhile and rested in the hush, I know that you are near and I can find myself again.

· In Thanks for a Friend ·

Lord Jesus, I thank you for my friend. We've known each other a long time and love each other in spite of faults and differences. We work together and play together and learn together. We trust each other with secrets, stand up for one another, and can be counted on when the going is hard.

Thank you, Lord, for this blessing, and help me to be a good friend.

· TO TRY ·

If I am not very good at something it is so easy
to forget about it, or to say that I don't like it,
or just not try very hard.

I give up too easily, God. Help me to try more,
to try without holding back and without fear of
failure. And when I do fail, help me to try
again with courage and lightness of heart.

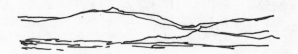

• LEARNING •

God, sometimes it is exciting to learn new
things, and I thank you for the chance. But
there are other times when learning seems to
be just dull and endless work. Help me then,
God. Teach me how to concentrate and to be
patient. Remind me of the good feeling of a
hard job well done and of the new possibilities
ahead when I have finished with the work I
must do first.

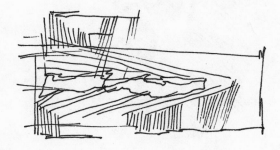

· My Body ·

You gave me my body, Christ. Help me to take care
of it and treat it as your creation and your dwelling.

· WORKING TOO HARD ·

O God of the Sabbath, I work too much. Work is good and necessary and I thank you for it, but I need to play more. I need to rest and relax, to walk and run, see friends and enjoy myself.

Remind me, God, to take time off, and help me not to feel guilty when I do.

· THE PAIN OF OUR NEIGHBORS ·

Jesus, Lord of all compassion, you told the story
of the good Samaritan who helped the man by
the side of the road. But today the city streets are
lined with scores of people in trouble and the
news brings stories and pictures of the pain and
problems of thousands more. It assaults my mind
and heart, Lord, and I want to forget them all.

O Jesus, stop me from closing my heart because I
am unable to help everyone. And guide the
compassion you have given me to help those you
wish me to help.

· FOR THE HUNGRY AND · THE HOPELESS

O Lord, in many places that I seldom or never see there are people hungry and without hope. Sometimes because I am not near them I forget and because I have not felt their troubles they don't seem real. But when I stop and dare to think, I know that they are real.

Lord, help these people whom I do not know and help me to help them. Give them strength and hope and take away their despair.

• AT THE END OF A BAD DAY •

O Father, I hurt inside tonight. Nothing has
gone the way it should. I didn't do very well and
people thought I did even worse than I did.
Take the tiredness away from me, God, and
make me feel all in one piece again. Show me
what I should do to make things better. Then let
your peace descend on my heart so I can sleep
well and get up tomorrow with your happiness
upon me, ready to do better.

· TO BE PATIENT WITH MY ·
MOTHER AND FATHER

God, sometimes it is easier to love people who
are not as close to you as your parents. I've always
expected my mother and father to be perfect,
and I get angry and hurt when they are not. I
depend on them when I should be independent,
and rebel when I should listen. And sometimes I
just close them out because I don't know what
else to do.

Help me, God, to understand and accept them as
they are. And help them to accept me as I am.

· FEAR ·

God, I am afraid. Not just of one thing but of many. It is not panic, just a quiet fear that has crept into places where I usually walk unafraid and is standing between me and people who wish me no harm. There is good reason for some of the fear, God. But most of it is unreal. I know this and yet I cannot seem to throw it off. And whether real or imagined, it makes me less able to be myself.

Take this fear from me, God, that I may move freely in your world and be more nearly the person you wish me to be.

◆ PRIDE AND CONFIDENCE ◆

I get confused, God. You have given me new confidence and I am grateful. But what is the difference between self-confidence and the kind of pride you don't want us to have? I'm not used to my new confidence, God. Help me to learn to use it and guide my thoughts and words.

• WHEN SOMEONE HAS DIED •

O Christ, someone I loved very much has died and there is an empty place I cannot fill. My heart aches and inside I feel stiff and tired.

Help me to remember that *she* is with you. And, O Christ, help me to be unafraid to walk the earth without *her* and to take strength and comfort from your love.

· MOURNING ·

He is gone. *His* pain is over and *he* is gone.
The funeral is over and the family and friends
have left. The letters are answered. But the
emptiness remains. The emptiness and so
much more. I am angry, God. I am angry at
him for dying and angry at you for letting *him*
die. I am angry at friends, who have been so
kind, because they are alive and because those
they love are alive.

I am angry too because I failed *him* so often. I
hurt *him.* I was selfish, thoughtless, mean. And
now *he* is gone, and I cannot undo the past.

It might be easier to pretend I am not angry
but I cannot fool you, God. Help me through
this time of anger and pain, of guilt and loss.
Help me to live as he — and you — would like
me to live.

· TO BE OLD ·

How to make these last days count, God? To
live them with courage, and without complaint.
To give and receive small joys. To teach the best
already learned and to learn a little more.

Nearer to you, we are more helpless; without
you, more lonely for you.

• I MAY NOT GET WELL •

Always, before this, I've just been sick for a while, a few days or a week or so. Once it was a matter of months. But now I realize that I may not get well. I may have to live with this pain until I die and come to you.

I don't want to face that, God. Neither pain that doesn't go away, nor death. I know that they come to us all, but I am not ready — not anywhere near ready.

Help me, God. Give me the hope, the patience and the courage that I need. Help me not to be too envious of those who are well. Take away my anger and resentment so that I don't hurt those around me. Help me to use my reduced energies and opportunities to the best of my ability. And above all, give me greater love and understanding for my family, my friends, and all those I see from day to day.

• CREATION •

God, sometimes I hold something small in my
hand, a piece of moss or a budding twig and,
peering closely at this tiny world, I feel a
sudden wonder. Help me to remember that
you made these worlds and countless others
and, in remembering, come closer to you.

· A QUIET TIME ·

O God, help me to learn to be still before you,
to take time to be with you quietly, without
talking or wishing to talk.

• ON THE USE OF TALENTS •

Help me to use the brains
that you have given me
without conceit, the hands
that you have given me
without laziness, and the
tongue you have given me
without hurting others.

· THE FAMILY OF GOD ·

I am alone but not alone, and I am grateful.
Not only are you with me, God, but so, in spirit,
are all that great company of people who try to
follow you. Even living near me there are
people I don't know who love you as I love you.
Every time I try and fail and am forgiven and try
again, I feel the unseen companionship of
many other people.

You have a family, God, and I am a part of your
family. It gives me strength and comfort to
remember this, and I thank you.

• How Large is Your Love •

O Lord, how large is your love!

My heart sings to you and the stones beneath my feet and the sky above my head sing also. All around me is your world and I know that you know all of it and it knows your love.

My thoughts leap at the wonder of it. It is all yours, from the little stones at my feet to the unending sky above.

O Lord, such a great knowing you have beyond counting, and such a great loving beyond measure! And I am caught up in it and sing of it to the world and to you.

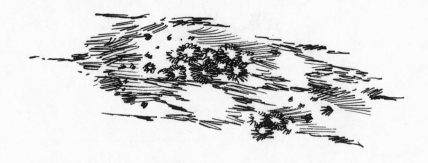

• HAPPINESS •

Sometimes happiness comes, unsought, unexpected and unearned. All around me life is bright. I love you, I love people, I even love myself. Work is play, and peace and joy dance together. Help me then, God, to use this blessing well, to share it and not keep it to myself.

· AN EVENING PRAYER ·

Father, I have much to be grateful for tonight, and I thank you. I have much to regret and I ask your forgiveness. But even as I ask your forgiveness I know that I receive it, and a deep peace fills my heart. Help me to sleep well tonight and to wake ready for that daily yet greatest of gifts, a fresh start.